ZO[
AVOIDANCE

MAGGIE SAWKINS

CinnamonPress
INDEPENDENT INNOVATIVE INTERNATIONAL

GW01451447

Published by Cinnamon Press
Meirion House,
Glan yr afon,
Tanygrisiau,
Blaenau Ffestiniog,
Gwynedd, LL41 3SU
www.cinnamonpress.com

The right of Maggie Sawkins to be identified as author of this work has been asserted by her in accordance with the Copyright, Designs and Patent Act, 1988. Copyright © 2015 Maggie Sawkins ISBN: 978-1-909077-96-6

British Library Cataloguing in Publication Data. A CIP record for this book can be obtained from the British Library.

Designed and typeset in Palatino by Cinnamon Press
Cover from an original design by i-i design Used with kind permission

Printed in Poland

Cinnamon Press is represented in the UK by Inpress Ltd www.inpressbooks.co.uk and in Wales by the Welsh Books Council www.cllc.org.uk

Acknowledgements

The title poem *Zones of Avoidance* was developed as a live literature production with Mark C Hewitt of LLL Productions. It received a Grants for the Arts award from Arts Council England and won the 2013 Ted Hughes Award for New Work in Poetry.

My Daughter's Habit, The Cord, The Night the Trees Fell Down, Folie a Deux, A Visual Exploration of Fetish and *Hooked*, were made into filmpoems by Abigail Norris. They can be seen at www.zonesofavoidance.wordpress.com

I am indebted to Mark C Hewitt for his vision and faith in my story. I also thank Danny Sullivan and John McCarthy from Portsmouth's Recovery Community, and the following individuals for sharing their testimonies: Vanessa Brown, Ryan Coles, Elliot Cranston, Lizzie Gradidge, Nathan Ingram, Kieran Judge, Dave Malcolm, Jason Marshall and Mark MacKay.

Work from this book has appeared in: *Ariadne's Thread, Beyond Stigma* (Barry Tebb, editor), *Brittle Star, Coal City Review, Did I Tell You?, Lyrical Beats, Magma, Obsessed with Pipework, South, Tall-lighthouse Review, The Butcher's Dog, The Zig Zag Woman* (Two Ravens Press), and Brittle Star's *Said and Done Anthology*.

As If I Could Replace the Weight of Her, Bronzefield, Come Back My Love, Our House, Retreat and *The Cord*, and have been placed or shortlisted in competitions.

Contents

One

Two

For

Grandsons –
Elliot Salvador and Michael Vasile

Zones of Avoidance

One

The dead drug leaves a ghost behind.
At certain times it haunts the house.
Jean Cocteau

Zones of Avoidance

I'm reading *The Confessions of an English Opium Eater* –
I want to understand what drove my daughter out in the snow

with no coat or socks, in search of a fix.
I want to understand what divinity led her

to set up camp in the derelict 'pigeon house'
after running out of sofas to surf.

*

I was a *Lucy in the Sky with Diamonds* girl myself.
I liked the way it made inanimate objects move

until that day in Balham when my guy sang *Rock n Roll Suicide*
from a third floor window and an Alsatian leapt

from the wood grain of the station door
and policemen were penguins in disguise.

*

Tough Love. The mantra of the support group
for those beaten by their loved one's addiction.

When I was busted at nineteen and the bedsit landlord
tipped my belongings onto the street, the last person

I would've turned to was my mother.
You've made your bed. Lie on it. Lie on it. Lie on it.

My mother warned me about heroin, but it wasn't to be
my drug of choice –

I preferred to turn on, tune in, drop out to Timothy Leary,
pick up my needle and move to another groove,

to fathom Hell and soar angelic,
to take a pinch of psychedelic.

*

My mother, who never touched a drop,
was addicted to cleaning,

as if she could tidy the scraps of unhappiness stashed
in the corner of her orphaned heart.

My father's solace for his bi-polar was brandy and soda,
laced with a medicinal dose of ECT.

*

De Quincy believed no-one, having tasted the divine
luxuries of opium, would afterwards

descend to *the gross and mortal enjoyments of alcohol.*
These days it's my only poison.

A glass of laudanum negus, warm and without sugar,
was his.

Opium pills coated in varnish for the labouring classes.
Others coated in silver and gold popped by the rich.

Mothers who quelled their babies with Ayers Cherry Pectoral and
Godfrey's Cordial chose to ignore the wisdom of

the Family Physician: *Those who would use opium for every ache
and pain would take an 80 ton gun to shoot a rabbit.*

*

The inebriate. The addict. The morphinomaniac –
the Victorian terminology for those hooked on God's own medicine.

Christian evangelists regarded addiction as a sin
born from the story of Adam and Eve.

*Treat them with scalding baths, mustard plasters
and physical force. Apply with contempt.*

*

Black Mamba, White Ivory, China White, Special K,
Yaba, Gumdrops,Purple Wave, Vanilla Sky –

the hedonist shop at the end of the road
has it all –

interesting gifts, seeds, pipes, aphrodisiacs and Shrooms,
weird stuff like 'I can't believe it's not heroin'.

Who can blame them? The crackheads, the speedfreaks,
the dipsomaniacs. Isn't this what we crave - to turn off

and on at will? The night is flying. I'm lying under the weight of
my eyes replaying the cameo of my daughter picking up dog ends

from the pavement after yesterday's matinee of Cinderella.
I'm imagining a face for the Higher Power.

*

I wake up wondering what it's like to cluck.
De Quincy said that when he tried to stop his eccentric pastime

it was as if rats were abrading the lining of his stomach.
Though filled with *torpor and stagnation, animal and mental,*

he carried on until he was forced to untwist, almost to its final links,
the accursed chain which fettered him.

*

Higher Power. What cave do you live in?
What clothes do you wear?

What makes you more than the spent rocket I found
on my doorstep on New Year's Day?

What would I give to believe in you? To rest my hand on yours
as it hovers above the switch attached to my core.

In 1863 Mrs Colebrook of Southsea ran a home for fallen women.
There was a society that gave blankets to the poor

and another that dished up dinners to delicate children.
Last week the Salvation Army made a plea in the paper

for disused sleeping bags for those of us who scavenge
the bins behind Iceland at midnight.

*

Mill House. A hostel for those who've been through the mill.
I've come to visit my daughter.

I follow as she limps along the corridor on high red heels.
She's babbling so much I don't have to say a word.

We reach her room where her new boyfriend's hiding.
He has tiny ears and a face carved in old wounds.

*

Waldo, the Peruvian support worker,
says his favourite poet's Pablo Neruda.

We're pondering over an *Ode to a Conger Eel*
when a resident keels over in the corridor.

A bottle spills and rolls to our feet.
Waldo rushes to lift him, as if his arms could hold a wave.

I don't know how I did it. Turned the particles of my soul
into a stone that could not be moved.

How I watched from my car as she scurried
into a derelict building at midnight.

God. If you exist you must be something small and solid
lodged like a silver bullet in the barrel of the heart.

*

I drive past the pigeon house – the place where
my grandson was most likely conceived.

They were happy there for a while, until the day
of the demolition.

Once I was even invited to tea, though I had to take
my own sandwiches, garibaldi biscuits and flask.

*

A cloud has entered the house.
We can neither pack it nor unpack it.

It has robbed us of lightness,
nudged us into corners, disturbed our vision.

You can't do battle with a cloud.
Its disdain for words will lose you ground.

I was hooked up once to a Guardian Angel
like the one I'd seen in a book.

Its wings tinged with fire lit up the blue sky
of my page. Back then God was a face in a cloud

and I believed in Heaven, and Hell
was just a word.

*

She's become unfathomable – my daughter who was fire.
I sit on the shingle surrounded by sea kale,

yellow-horned poppy, plants with roots anchored
below the surface. It's unnatural for one

made of flesh and bone to be so unmovable.
It will take an earthquake to break her.

*

Papavar Somniferum, guardian of eternal sleep,
who made you?

Once exposed to the sun, your milky sap
turns to opium black.

Is this our destination, this place where hope
has lost its wings?

I want to remember her, carrying a sandcastle bucket
full of crabs, wearing the bolero my mother made.

Never one to shy away from a crash of waves,
she's walking straight into the sea.

A stranger on the beach alerts me.
Always at the last minute I rush in to save her.

*

The baby's father's Romanian, no fixed abode.
My daughter thinks he can fix her life,

as if love was more than a sleight of hand.
This morning I clocked him staggering in flip-flops

towards the cemetery in Highland Road.
If he's in luck, tonight, Securicor won't move him on.

*

The tick and the tock. All the echoing corridors
in between. So this is where they were leading –

to this spot that frames us in strip-light
waiting for a nurse to unlock the door,

where we listen, stricken, to the words *I love you*
escaping from the hard box of my throat.

The Taurus Void is large and circular.
Walls of galaxies surround it.

Is this where she's hiding? My daughter
and her baby boy born under the sign of the bull.

Is this where he'll come looking one day
with his scrap-paper past curled in his fist?

*

The day my daughter agreed to have her baby adopted,
a torso was found in a bag on the beach.

The pebbles in front of Rocksby's Café are strewn
with blue disposable gloves, numbered yellow cones.

What's to distinguish a person who's lost their face,
their hands, the gaze reflected in a mother's eye?

*

I like to think the heart doesn't keep growing.
That when it's cut from the body and placed on the scales

it weighs no more than a newborn's.
I like to think of it rising from the surgeon's hands

(as the Egyptians believed it would)
to find its place in Heaven.

Euphoria. You razor-edged friend.
You've robbed your devotees of the gift of grief.

Is this your mission – a one-way ticket
to an unknown zone?

Anonymous as waves. Is this what we become
when no-one is looking?

*

The baby's been appointed a guardian.
In dreams I watch as he's sent from nest to nest

and each time I forget to pack his feed.
A dog with two masters will starve to death,

or so the dictum goes. Four months on
and my daughter's still secreting milk.

*

The court rises for Judge Marsh. He glances down
at the legal guardian and us,

says this is one of the saddest cases,
becoming a grandparent should be a time of joy.

The interpreter repeats the gist of it
in the baby's father-tongue.

An owl is perched on the end of my bed.
I follow as it flies downstairs and into the lounge

where it settles on some plumped-up cushions.
It opens its beak and tries to speak.

My daughter arrives from the garden
with three dead mice.

*

We've made the baby a memory book.
Inside's a photo of my daughter struggling

to push his newborn arm into a sleeve.
There's a skeleton of his family tree.

We're to be allowed letterbox contact –
we'll compose our words faceless as stars.

*

The day we drove to the adoption centre in Hester Road
it was zero degrees.

My daughter sang along to Prince's *Purple Rain*, as if her voice
could drown out fate. We hugged the baby goodbye.

I dropped her off at Baytrees to begin her detox.
If she ever meets him again he'll be a little man.

A weekend's leave from rehab, but she's not permitted
to stay with me

because I drink wine with my evening meal. Three glasses
of Pinot Grigio. My passport

to intimacy. It makes me smile to think
I'm out of bounds.

*

It's Day Two of her job at the King Prawn Takeaway.
She's stopped by after her shift for a cup of tea.

Topics of conversation: Romanian culture, bleeding,
ugly boyfriends, the Chinese, and suicide.

She believes some of us are born with the right to take
our own lives. But she's not one of them.

*

We're in the garden, Sunny Girl and me, sipping Cola,
talking about everything and nothing,

No longer boxing at shadows, no longer knocking back
tears.

The wind's chasing leaves from the handkerchief tree –
the branches are losing their grip.

Folie à Deux

At first the changes in their behaviour
will alarm you. They will accuse you, for instance,
of trying to kill them by spooning amounts
of salt into their food. They will develop
headaches and you'll find it difficult
to believe, at first, that this is a result
of your evil thoughts. You'll fail to hear the whispers
on the television & radio as they interrupt
the news to tell of your grandmother's
recent abduction. Then, one day, you'll notice
that the television & radio have disappeared.
The telephone also will become a subject
of consternation. It too will disappear.

You will use your powers of reason, then
you will stop. You'll spend your days on tip-toe,
emptying ashtrays, making cups of tea,
contacting the authorities from the telephone box
at the end of the road. You will learn that to argue
is not an option. You will remove your display
of kitchen knives, forget how to sleep. You'll begin
to gaze at the space between stars.

Then, slowly, all the minutes and the hours and the days
of the past months will slot into place. You'll shave off
your eyebrows, pluck your hair, stop answering
the door. You'll realise the Prime Minister
really is a drug addict who uses our taxes
to fund his habit, and the neighbour
from Albania who poisoned your dog,
is wearing its coat as a hat.

The Real Thing

Sunday morning. The doorbell rings. I put on my dressing gown and go down. Sitting on the doorstep, with her back to me, is Sunny Girl. She gets up and I let her in. She's wearing three overcoats, she's dyed her blonde hair black, she's spent the whole night walking.

Three weeks later and I'm driving along Waverley Road looking for number 42. It's a guest house called *Avalon*. I take the bin bag of clothes from the boot and ring the bell. The landlord tells me she's in a room at the top of the stairs.

She's lying on the bed watching *Who Wants to be a Millionaire?* I sit down and she asks what the other night was about. The other night. The night the police came to evict her from my mother's eighth floor flat. 'I don't know,' I say. 'Nan said she couldn't cope with you being there.' Silence, as she sifts through the bag of clothes.

'I have to go soon,' I say. But she starts talking. Tells me about Glasgow and the railway station that turned into a ship, how she told them about it at the hospital but they just laughed. She said she was sitting in a room opposite Bin Laden when a guard came in and told her she was going to be tagged to stop her travelling without paying the fare.

She's laughing now. I look up. The contestant on *Who Wants to be a Millionaire* has just lost thirty two thousand because he doesn't know who wrote *The Return of the Native*. 'You'd better tell the Americans,' I say, 'they're bombing the wrong place.'

I get up to go but she carries on talking. Tells me how the police turfed her out of the station at midnight, how she walked to Petersfield and slept on a bench. She shows me the boots she bought a month ago. She'd spent a whole week's incapacity benefit on them. The heels are worn down and the soles have holes. I offer to take them to the shop for mending.

I go home. Pick up the book I've been reading – it's about a man who's lost his daughter. I bought it because I wanted something to relate to but I can't. It seems too clever, too full of words. I think the author doesn't really know what it's like to lose a child – it's just an artifice, not the real thing.

I pick up the bundle of poems given to me by one of my students, a self-harmer. It's full of abstractions, packed with clichés – all the crimes a creative writing teacher tells you not to commit. But it's full of feeling – straight from the gut, and reading it makes me cry.

Unread Stories

I'll spare you the blow by blow account of Christmas Day, but you'll know what I mean when I say Sunny Girl had her stormy head on. She'd spent all her benefits and won't get anything now till Tuesday. That's five days with no money for food, baccy, or a fix.

It started in the kitchen. She was sat at the table muttering and making faces. When she realised I wasn't going to cough up, she was shouting and making her way to the door. I told her to clear off, she whacked me in the face with her Davy Crockett hat, I shoved her, she kicked me and left, slamming the door. More of a cat than a dog fight.

I took Buster for a walk along the seafront. The day had a bite to it. There seemed to be more people on their own than usual and a young Asian guy wished me Merry Christmas.

No-one can see into your past. We walk around like unread stories and here I was already rewriting the events of the day. Realising I'd moved on. I was no longer afraid to say no.

Back in the kitchen and our friend Jack's arrived and Ted's set the table for three, instead of four. Then the phone rings. It's Sunny Girl sounding calmer, enquiring whether she's still invited to dinner. I ask if she's in a better frame of mind. Ted demands an apology. Two minutes later she's at the door, armed with three orange roses.

In the end, you'll be pleased to hear, it was a good day. We argued over the duck and made up over the crackers. In the evening another friend arrived and we sat talking till midnight - though Sunny Girl did most of it. The gear she'd managed to get hold of had done the trick.

She told us about the night she'd spent sleeping under Jacob's Ladder, a bridge in Somers Town, and about her pet angel fish that liked to play football. She said that since she'd become a meat eater she could pack a punch.

It's difficult to tell what's true and what's a delusion. I guess I ended up thinking she was more eccentric than insane. She was wearing a long tiger print dress over the thermal leggings I'd bought her, and a pair of Cinderella slippers.

When it was time to go, she put on the old flying jacket our friend Alan had given her to keep her warm, and her Davy Crockett hat. She gave us all a kiss goodbye and left - thanking us for a lovely day.

Sub Title: *A Visual Exploration of Fetish*

Sunny Girl's hollering through the letterbox.
It's my birthday. I follow the tail
of her Davy Crockett hat down the hall.
She hands me a glossy hardback:
Doris Kloster's *Demimonde*

'Quick! Look inside. There's a picture of you.'
I locate a dog-eared page and peer.
'It's not me.'
'Yes it is. What's up? Don't you like it?'
My head nods. My mouth smiles.
She kisses my hand and scoots.

I show Ted.
The woman in question is coupled
in a game of female bondage.
She's wearing red ankle boots and a thong.
He's impressed.
'Well … she does look a bit like you,
apart from that rose tattoo on her cheek …'

He returns to his Sunday paper.
I pore over the rest of the book.
On the centrefold there's an oldish man
in a leather pouch, all wrapped up in cling film.
In his mouth's an orange.

'I see the government's advocating free allotments
for the over fifties ...'
'It's not normal,' I say.

The Night the Trees Fell Down

found us rolling home after midnight from a gig
at *The Good Intent*, my pub singer partner
pointing a key at the door.
I'm right behind him, unsteady on my heels
and ready to crash. I tumble into the lounge.
On the sofa's Sunny Girl, lost to the world.
I ruffle her hair, call out her name,
but she barely moves. I kick over a can of Cola,
pick up an empty bottle of sleepers.

I locate the room on D wing.
Her stomach's been pumped. I hold on
to her hand, but I'm light years away.
I try to speak, but there's no lexicon
for this new language. That the windows
are rattling, that the strip lights flicker
as if possessed, all seems part of the show.
I watch the movement of her eyes behind their lids
until a nurse comes in, says I should go.

So I walk along the green corridors, follow the signs
for the exit, empty myself into the 3 a.m. air.

My Daughter's Habit

A month's respite doesn't stop the heart
tilting in its cradle at the knock,

the scene replayed before I open the door.
I know from her expression what she wants,

but still she asks, and I fetch,
like a dog, hand over the score,

notice once more the half-moon scar
on the bone of her cheek.

The night swallows her shadow,
catches my sigh as she walks away.

I lean a while against the door,
listen as the wind worries the trees,

smother the thought: to press
a pillow against my slipping heart.

Bronzefield

Sounds like a place that once
was torched
by the breath of a god,

but more likely it was built
on a field of corn,

this building with high red walls

where you've finally
been netted .

My mutant butterfly,
when I come to visit
they search my mouth.

Act

'This is what is hardest: to close the open hand because one loves.'
Friedrich Nietzsche

I wasn't cut out to be a Joan of Arc.
It was a mistake. My ears became immune

to the same old tune. I've made my choice,
shut the door, shunned the glory.

I've morphed you, my love, into a wolf
in kid's clothing, a baby-faced liar.

And though your howls infiltrate my dreams,
I will not stray from the path.

I'll recover my smile, reclaim my laugh.
Yes, I'm okay, since you inquire.

Except ... look here ... what's this?
Is this my soul? Is it on fire?

Hooked

I should lock you out but you're too far in
You curl up with me when I lie down
In dark places I hear you whimper
I dare not move in case you stir.

You curl up with me when I lie down
When morning breaks I try to leave you
I dare not move in case you stir
I feel you brush against my skin.

When morning breaks I try to leave you
You're just a creature by my side
I feel you brush against my skin
I vow each time not to feed you.

You're just a creature by my side
In dark places I hear you whimper
I vow each time not to feed you
I should lock you out but you're too far in.

The Cord

When I thought of what she was carrying
I imagined it the colour of silt,

and if it had eyes then they were the eyes
of a fish long out of water.

I imagined it soulless, like a stone
(a stone cannot haunt one's dreams),

so that if it was taken from us,
we'd be glad to be rid of it.

I hadn't reckoned for the sound
of its unborn heartbeat

that was the heartbeat of a colt
cantering towards grass

or when it came, its mewl –
the physicality of detachment.

When the nurse asked if I would cut it,
I could not cut it.

Dear Boy

I was there the moment you were born, along with the three psychiatric nurses who cheered you on. We watched the midwife place you on the scales. You weighed 5lbs 15oz and your head was blue! I took a photograph of your birth mother struggling to fit you into your yellow baby grow. I imagined it the last thing she would do for you, and I thought I was going to cry.

When I visited you the next day in the neo-natal unit you looked a lot better and the nurse let me cradle you for a while. You were how I imagined you would be - your skin the colour of sand and your eyes shut tight.

Two weeks later your birth father called round to our house. I printed off the directions for the place where he was to see you for the first time. He was so excited. He had some clothes for you and a Mickey Mouse doll made of cloth.

When I was little my mum used to say, *'When poverty walks in the door, loves flies out the window.'* Your birth mother and father loved each other and they loved you, but they had so many problems it was impossible for them to keep you.

Your birth father came from a family of farmers in Southern Romania. His mother left the family when he was thirteen, so he had to leave school to work on the farm. Romania's a poor country with little opportunity for young people. When he was eighteen he wanted to see the world, thinking he could make a living in another country. So he made his way to Italy and from there to Ireland where he worked on the land before coming to London.

But it was difficult to find work there, so he decided to go back to Romania. Someone told him he would need to get a boat from Portsmouth, so he walked all the way from London. It took him six days. Can you imagine that?

While he was walking along the motorway near to the ferry port he was stopped by the police who took him to a hostel for homeless people in Portsmouth, and that's where he met your birth mother. Even though they had nowhere permanent to stay they looked after each other.

After your birth your mother went back to the psychiatric intensive care unit. She was allowed to visit you for half an hour a day until you went to stay with your foster carers. She so wanted to get well so that she could look after you, but it wasn't to be.

Boy, you were the son of sleep and the brother of fantasy. One day you will make someone else's dreams come true.

Dear Boy

I met your new parents last week. You'll be going home with them on St Valentine's Day - it feels like a good omen.

Your birth mother was with me. I'd picked her up from the hospital where she's being detoxed. It was her second day without any methadone and she was feeling shivery and sick. Methadone's a powerful drug that doctors give to people who've become addicted to heroin. It's meant to stop the craving. Heroin's an illegal drug - though some people think it would be better if it wasn't, so that it could be controlled like alcohol. Maybe when you're older the situation will be different and addiction will be treated as a medical issue and not a crime.

I feel honoured to have met your new parents. I was so pleased to hear they have a puppy and that your new dad fixes engines. It sounds like your childhood's going to be lots of fun! But it was a strange day. It was like when people meet relatives they didn't know existed - except this was in reverse. This was like meeting strangers who've become your instant family. Though we might not see each other again, we'll always be connected, just like the moon is to the sea.

We hoped we'd be able to have a photo of you now and again, to see you growing up. But that's not to be. But I imagine sometimes we'll catch sight of a boy when we're out, shopping or at the seaside, and we'll wonder whether it could be you.

Boy, your coming was a good thing. Your birth mother's begun to turn her life around. She's taken a big step by going into rehab. Perhaps if it wasn't for you she may never have found the strength. If she'd carried on with the life she was leading, there's even a possibility that she might not have lived much longer. I was prepared for that - more so than your birth! You've helped our family come together again, and I'm grateful for that.

...

Soon it will be your first birthday.
I will light a candle and make a wish.

'Higher Power, wherever you're hiding,
please fill this boy's life with new moons.
Endless bright stars.

Two

In the struggle between yourself and the world,
hold the world's coat.
Kafka

The World's Coat

The world's coat
has a zillion buttons made of stone,

has pockets
deeper than the Pacific Ocean;

with its collar pulled up
it reaches beyond the death of stars.

Its fabric can cope with hurricane and hail,
sandstorm and snow;

it can embrace your sorrows and your fears
of no tomorrow.

The world's coat is lined with silk from all the silk worms
that ever existed;

its length is long but it never touches the ground.
There's no reason to shun it –

it is waiting patient as the sky for you to sink
into the black holes of its arms.

The world's coat
may seem an ill fit, but just turn up

its cuffs, it will grow into you,
or you into it.

Title: *Come Back My Love*

That night I met Darts backstage I was high,
not on jungle juice, just the fizz –
me being asked along by *The Flying Post's* chief reporter
to interview my favourite band. Bob Fish kissed
my hand and Rita Ray gave me a signed copy
of their LP.

I knew nothing then about sections or dual diagnosis,
the steps you must take to visit your loved one
in a women's prison. I'd only been married once,
to some guy from Balham who had a bedside lamp
called Plato, and even though I'd read
Crime and Punishment and Wilson's *Outsider,*
I knew nothing about keeping knives
tidied away in kitchen drawers.

I hadn't done anything much. Never picked up
a piece of the Berlin Wall, smelt fruit bats
from a Port Douglas veranda at midnight,
seen the way trees in the rain forest
strangle each other.

But that night I knew all about doo wop,
that night I was attraction,
that night I didn't wash my hand.

A Cage Went in Search of a Bird

Kafka

What use is a cage
that's become afraid

of its own trappings –
its mirror, its bell, its swing?

What use is an opening
that doesn't stay open?

What use is a perch
that doesn't stay still?

No use thinking things
will change

should a bird fly in
and make itself at home.

What use is a companion
if your fear's so loud

you cannot hear
their song?

The Year the Wall Came Down

I found myself in No Man's Land. Sir took a photograph of me posing in front of twisted stanchion and rubble. A few yards away people were sitting behind trestle tables selling fragments of the wall. I picked a piece marked with faded red paint from the ground. Perhaps once it had been the upstroke of a stranger's name.

In the afternoon Sir took us to the museum. I stayed the whole time in Caspar David Friedrich's room looking at a painting of a monk standing on the edge of a vast still sea. It was so unlike home where waves crashed against walls.

After supper I stood in the queue by the telephone kiosk, then wandered into the hostel bar. Apart from *herr barmann*, the room was empty. I caught a glimpse of a young woman in the mirror opposite, her eyes another country. She was staring straight through me to a place without a corners – a place where no-one knew your scent, your name.

The Wild Mouse

There they are!
My mother and father
chugging along
the high-rise track
   in their little red car.

She's sitting behind him,
her legs drawn up –
the wind's whipped
   candy floss into her hair.

I can see the back
of my father's white shirt,
his tattooed hands
   gripping the bar.

Soon they'll reach the bit
where the nose of the car
juts out over the sea –
my mother will close her eyes and scream.

Then the car will jack-knife
on its rickety rail,
dive down
and down
as if to crash
   right into the crowd.

As they whizz past
I'll look up and wave
(my heart's on my sleeve!),
but they'll be holding on so tight
   they will not see.

Misnomer

That's not my mother
My mother was a gypsy with corkscrew hair.
She made cucumber dragons, tickled my hand,
raced me on dodgems, played Spanish guitar.

That's not my mother.
My mother had a face like a moon in a bottle.
She picked bluebells and blackberries,
taught me to hula, pierced my ears.

That woman has cropped hair
and eyes like glass. She's come with pyjamas,
and moccasins and tortoiseshell comb. She stares
at my face. She talks about home.

My gypsy mother's sent a card –
a white horse in a field with its mane flying.
Inside she's left three spidery kisses,
but she's forgotten to leave her name.

Episode

/she's phoning to tell me
that she was last seen
in *The Empty Fish*

with a bunch of keys
and a photograph
of her son

and if I find her
can I go to her flat
the bunch of keys

are important
because they're the keys
to her room

in her room
are her papers and her records
of missing people

and when I see her
I might be shocked
because she's gone to bone

she's not sure
what's safe to eat
anymore

she's been pregnant twice
but no-one believes her
she's heard the babies talking

the babies know
about the missing people
she thinks she may be missing too/

Seeing Things

That was the year I saw them everywhere –
around tree tops and roofs, cyclists on pavements,
bin men and doctors, even dogs in the park.

And I couldn't stop smiling. Though in truth
there was little to make me smile –
my father confined after his episode

with the purple heart cocktail, my mother's
outings to The Royal for radiation –
and topping it all, me being dropped a class

for spending too much time listening
to Dr Baraduc of Bordeaux's recordings
of thought vibrations. That was the year

I discovered the vulture headed god, Ma-at,
whose third eye was the eye of the soul;
and the year Barbara Skinner, the only girl

without an aura, socked me. It was the year
of still believing and the of year of not knowing
the dangers of staring straight at the sun.

Wall

I'm tempted to knock
a nail into your silence,
disturb your smugness

with an old bevelled mirror
or Goya's painting
of the disconsolate dog –

but I won't. No –
I will sit in the lotus
like a yogi before you,

contemplate
your pin-pocked plainness,
instruct my bones

in the art of stillness,
cast from my memory
my father's hunched shoulders,

my mother's lost hat.
I'll sit there so long,
my nails will yellow and curl

and you'll begin to moulder;
until the day that you, me, the world
and its dog

transmute into an echoless blue –
so what do you say
to that?

Our House

Don't think it was all *Shut it!*
in our house.

Go back to the time when the dog
was sick

and they nursed him all night
with sips of brandy,

to when snow filled the yard
and I was sent out

with mash and bran for Bobtail
the rabbit,

to the sprigs of chickweed we picked
for the budgie

and the seed and lard ball tied to the tree
with string.

Don't think when they died
no-one cared,

the grief couldn't get past the gate,
that's all.

Gripped

Lean against the wall
by the shuttered
ice-cream kiosk

watch the huge balloon
that's settled
on the horizon

its tail of crimson light
trailed like a ragged
ribbon across

the surface of the sea.
Hold on
until all that's left

is a cuticle of red
then you let go
as if it were nothing

Destination: Port of New York –
23 December 1929

Even though your name is there
on the SS Cameronia's passenger list:
Regina M Keohane, scholar aged eight,
of sound mind and body,
you were the one sister
left behind in Aughnacliffe
along with your Granda's blue cow
and your milk bottle doll.

But if you had gone
I would not have been born,
I wouldn't have spent my life
caught in an undertow,
watching for the feathering of waves,
fighting the weight of an ocean.

The Drowners

They will step
into you –
first a toe, then
the ball of a foot.
Some will come clothed,
though most will leave
something behind –
a tell-tale coat,
a pair of shoes.
They will make it
seem easy, as if
they are stepping
into nightfall –
not even you,
nor the eye of a god,
will be able to stop them.
All you can do is slip
momentarily aside,
witness the last
bubbles of breath,
and then they are yours.
You may wonder
what panacea they think
you possess –
but you'll be out
of your depth.
All you can do
is offer up your home,
knowing that even if
the world tipped
itself sideways –
words will not spill
from your mouth.

Stone Maquette

I caught your eye. Something about me
put you in mind of someone long gone,
perhaps it's this hole that once was heart.

Being nothing, I ask for nothing,
my weight is a sort of miracle.
Sculpt these hollows into what you will.

I won't laugh or shriek – I have no tongue,
no legs to run, no hands to strangle
or stroke or tickle you in your sleep.

Keep me as a charm, a silent muse –
don't try to talk to me, what's the use?
I cannot hear – I've been dead too long.

As if I Could Replace the Weight of Her

ghost lights skim the sky as she steps from sleep
into the tundra

I watch as she lifts her hands to the falling snow – stop
where she stops

shocked into stillness at the sighting of an arctic fox
its fur blue-white

vanishing into the vast outreach
of nothing

back at the lodge I dream her dreams pray for huskies
to pull her through

come dawn I'll watch as she readies herself for home
tuck in her rucksack

a jar of yellow cloudberries, a miniature bottle
of strange liquor

after she's gone I'll step out of myself into the hollows
of her footprints

Antarctica to Tamazepam

When people asked what her problem was
she insisted *late nights* –

even though she tip-toed upstairs with her mug
of milk and manuka honey

and sprayed her bed with *Jujube Dreamy Pillow Spray*
and stopped her ears with yellow foam

against next door's miniature schnauzer
and recited all the places in the world

beginning and ending in A
until her head was a maze of A's

and practised the Zen of transmuting thoughts
into logs floating along the Yangtze River –

nothing worked. So now she reaches for the bottle
with the amazing name

and with a pill poised on the tip of her tongue
she unplugs her ears and waits for her thoughts

to dissolve like sugar cubes lobbed into
Yellowstone's Lone Star Geyser.

Papillon

What did it for him, he said,
after ten years relapsing,

was one of those wide-awake nights
at Eskimo's gaff down by *The Hard.*

That night it dawned on him that if
he needed a fix and all the stores

were closed and barred and if
there was no family round the corner –

he'd have the first passing stranger.
If there was a struggle, he said,

it wouldn't matter. If it cost a life,
it cost a life. He'd have to have it.

Till then, he said, he'd always
considered himself a moral thief –

would only steal from mates,
the old girl's purse,

his brother's Dalek money tin.
That's what did it for him.

Oh yeah, that, he said,
that and the late night film.

The dream scene. Steve McQueen
tramping through the desert,

dressed like a spiv to face the judge and jury.
Those words, he said:

I accuse you of a wasted life.
That's what did it for him.

Chasers

The morning after the concert party
I catch him pouring whisky into his tea.
He's talking poetry and women
the ones he's lost to horses and drink.
And because he reminds me
I tell him about my ex –
how when things got bad
he'd come back from the bookies
so flustered you'd think he'd been chasing
a horse by the name of *Love's Tail*
around the track.

He pours another Talisker's,
I sip my gin – think about
the years it takes to get out –
the split breath to fall in.

Visiting Mr U

i.m. of the real Graham Uttley

You won't remember me (or so I've been told) though
you seem to follow with your one good eye,
which leads me to think I'm more than a shadow.

You won't remember, then, when you took me
for a spin in your 1970's MGB,
me with my foot on your imaginary brake,
the maniac road disappearing under our seats;
or the rollover bar installed in the interests of safety,
or the gas struts fitted to the bonnet and boot,
the stainless steel exhaust that barely raised
a growl.

You won't remember, either, the day we took Treacle
for a walk on her three good legs,
how we stooped to pass through Market Needham's
cattle tunnel, the junk shop's biscuit barrel shaped like a pig.

Nor will you remember the pilfered gladioli you waved
from the aisle at Luke and Jo's orange-themed wedding,
your pairs of pink socks, your flair for cartoons
and satirical doodling.

You won't remember me (or so I've been told) though
I like to think the soul is more than a shadow;
see how it follows with its one good eye.

A Dog Asleep in the Crook of your Arm

who wouldn't crave an end like this
a suddenness

the world made calm
no brute force, no false alarm

no call to resist
just two sleepers in a tryst

a dog's sigh
its breath fur-warm

what better way to take your leave
an artless closing of the eye

life's tools gently dropped
a dog's head against your sleeve

the turning of a key
all sound end stopped.

The Dress

The white dress stained with red wine, now destined for the tip,
was the white dress worn to a wedding by the woman who,
preferring the magic of dogs, didn't feel the urge to marry.

The incident with the red wine didn't occur at the wedding
of the friend of the woman who preferred dogs, but when
the woman wore the white dress one winter to the wake of

an old soak in the drizzle-eyed County of Cork. It was the fate of
the white dress stained with red wine to outlive the woman
who, preferring the magic of dogs, & who wasn't destined

for wifehood, fell one day from a sleigh being pulled by
a fleet of sleet-eyed huskies, into the conjured snow of
the Finnmark Tundra in the friskiest year of her singular life.

The Emptiness

Then one day you'll carry the whole sack of it into the rain.

You'll carry it past houses with doors flung open
but you won't step in,
you'll carry it past trees
but you won't stop to shelter.

There'll be faded mansions on every corner with jukeboxes blaring,
there'll be canned laughter, crocodile tears,
but you'll carry on carrying it

past stray dogs lapping in sudden puddles,
past gamblers and loan sharks drowning in pop-up pools,
but you won't fall in.

You'll carry it with your eyes set beyond the horizon,
beyond the glass gaze of the sun

until you find the right spot to cast your sodden clothes
and you'll lay down your weight and your shadow beside it
and the rain will drain through you
and the rain will drain through you

About the Author

Maggie Sawkins is the founder of Portsmouth poetry and music club, Tongues&Grooves, set up in 2003 with the aim of empowering people to express themselves through writing and performance. Her poetry collections include *Charcot's Pet* (Flarestack) and *The Zig Zag Woman* (Two Ravens Press). Her work has been frequently anthologised and her articles on poetry and well-being are included in *Writing Your Self* (Continuum) and *Writing Routes* (Jessica Kingsley Publishers). In 2013 she was chosen by the Poetry Book Society to represent Portsmouth on the T. S. Eliot Poetry Prize Tour. The multimedia production of *Zones of Avoidance* directed by Mark C. Hewitt with video sequences by artist Abbie Norris and musical transitions by Portsmouth pedal steel guitarist, Nick Evans won the 2013 Ted Hughes Award for New Work in Poetry. Maggie is a qualified Peer Recovery Broker and trainer on Portsmouth City Council's 'Working Therapeutically with Addictions' course. She lives in Southsea, where she teaches creative writing in community and health care settings.

End Notes

Zones of Avoidance grew out of a sequence of poems inspired by the writer's personal and professional involvement with people in recovery from addictions and combines her own moving testimony with the voices of addicts in recovery. Featured at many festivals, the book accompanies the ambitious, award-winning multimedia performance of this brave and moving collection.